T0208173

CAREER FRUSTRATION
IN THE WORKPLACE

CAREER FRUSTRATION
IN THE WORKPLACE

Michael Owhoko

CAREER FRUSTRATION IN THE WORKPLACE

Copyright © 2016 Michael Honren Owhoko.

All rights reserved. No part of this book may be used or reproduced by
any means, graphic, electronic, or mechanical, including photocopying,
recording, taping or by any information storage retrieval system
without the written permission of the author except in the case of
brief quotations embodied in critical articles and reviews.

iUniverse books may be ordered through booksellers or by contacting:

iUniverse
1663 Liberty Drive
Bloomington, IN 47403
www.iuniverse.com
1-800-Authors (1-800-288-4677)

Because of the dynamic nature of the Internet, any web addresses or
links contained in this book may have changed since publication and
may no longer be valid. The views expressed in this work are solely those
of the author and do not necessarily reflect the views of the publisher,
and the publisher hereby disclaims any responsibility for them.

Any people depicted in stock imagery provided by Thinkstock are
models, and such images are being used for illustrative purposes only.
Certain stock imagery © Thinkstock.

ISBN: 978-1-4917-8552-2 (sc)
ISBN: 978-1-4917-8553-9 (e)

Library of Congress Control Number: 2015920670

Print information available on the last page.

iUniverse rev. date: 02/01/2016

Contents

Preface

Every professional who has risen through the ranks, or commenced his or her career and then risen to the top, has a story to tell – whether within the context of his or her personal experience, or in terms of understanding of others while in service. Some have pleasant and fulfilled careers, while others go through bitter and regrettable journeys in their quest for career fulfilment.

Having traversed three industries – namely, the media, banking, and oil and gas – it has always been my ambition to document and share my work experience with the general public. The scope of this book, however, will be limited to the frustrations most people encounter while in service. In other words, our discussion will focus on the work life of employees, identifying various obstacles which serve as direct threats to their career dreams. This exposition is just a reflection of what transpires among millions of employees worldwide.

Many employees all over the world suffer silent psychological trauma in the course of their employment, owing to unfulfilled career dreams. By no fault of their own, these individuals find themselves enmeshed in the bureaucratic politics of their organisations, which cast them as victims in some instances.

Since I was also a victim, it is important to describe my own experience, as well as what I observed of others' experiences. Sharing all these experiences will help to demystify the trend in modern offices and also help potential victims to overcome office politics and the bumper traps along their individual career paths.

How did I survive the experience? Throughout my career, I upheld certain principles and deployed specific methods which enabled me to cope with the circumstances in which I found myself. This book will explain and describe these principles and methods. The advice is particularly valuable for those who do not intend to establish their own business, but, rather, to take up a career as an employee in either the private sector or public service. However, even entrepreneurs and those who own their business will benefit from reading this book. The principles and methods described will also assist in analysing the nominal and operational disposition of employees towards work, and in assessing their basic character and personal make-up.

For the purposes of this book, I will refrain from mentioning the specific firms or companies in the three industries where I have worked. In a similar vein, I will leave off names of individuals, colleagues, subordinates, and superordinates with whom I have worked. This is obviously aimed at protecting the corporate image and reputation of these establishments, as well as the reputations of the individuals concerned. Put differently, it is imperative to protect the identities of these companies and persons in order to avoid any misinterpretations.

It is important to note that the experiences described in this book do not in any way single out the companies or organisations as culpable of the issues raised, as it has become almost a universal practice for managers in most companies to disconnect from organisational interests in an attempt to foster their own personal interests. In fact, they use their positions to bring their personal interests to bear on institutions. It may not be pronounced, but it is present in almost all organisations. While the majority of managers tend to follow through with this policy in the course of discharging their responsibilities, paradoxically, some others ensure that their vision and ideas, rather than those of the company, are pushed down their subordinates' throats. It is this category of managers that this book intends to address, as they abound everywhere.

Throughout the time of the experiences related in this book, I was restrained from petitioning higher authorities for fear that justice might not be objectively dispensed. Instead, I absorbed the pain and frustration and then resolved to concentrate my energies on writing and publishing a book depicting my experiences. I reasoned that it was better to commercialise my experience than to make an entreaty. Apart from the advantage of commercial gains, this book will further boost my profile as an author. (My first book, *The Language of Oil and Gas,* was published in 2010.)

Finally, I am eternally grateful to Almighty God for providing me with the opportunity to have worked in the three industries which served as the platforms for enabling me to get to where I am today. Without these organisations, putting this book together would have been knotty, if not impossible. In other words, this book is a product of my career passage.

[AUTHOR'S NOTE: Managers *and* supervisors *will be used interchangeably throughout this book; in addition, they also include the connotations of* general managers *and* managing directors. *Also,* bosses *will be used generically to refer to any and all of the foregoing.*]

Chapter 1

Organisational Vision, Goals, and Objectives

Every organisation or institution has a set of vision and mission statements which serve as a business compass for its aspiration and direction. Owing to the importance of these statements, they are conspicuously displayed in strategic positions in organisations. This allows them to be ever visible to all stakeholders, reminding them of the direction the company is headed within the context of its overall existence.

Similarly, goals are critical in the life of every organisation. They are an integral part of every organisation, clearly defining the company's ambitions in terms of what it wants to achieve, at what particular time, and with which required resources (whether human or material, and whether currently possessed or needing to be acquired). In addition to overarching goals, there are short-, medium-, and long-term smaller goals, which are periodically reviewed to ascertain the level of achievement within a particular period.

These are the parameters upon which companies and organisations are built. In all the years of my career, which spanned more than thirty years in three industries (the media, banking, oil and gas, as mentioned in the preface), the foregoing provided the basic structure for each organisation.

Colleagues, friends, and associates whose views I have sought on this issue have also confirmed it. Even those with heterogeneous experiences and backgrounds, whom I also queried in the course of writing this book, also corroborated this position. Besides, senior personnel in other industries whose views I also pursued confirmed the objectives of vision and mission statements. Indeed, organisational goals are vehicles through which the future of organisations revolves. In other words, the prospects of an organisation are predicated upon the goals.

It is therefore certain that for an organisation or institution to thrive in business, a clear set of vision and mission statements, as well as corporate goals and objectives, must be clearly defined and put in place.

Ironically, despite the importance of the foregoing, some companies are unable to follow through with their vision and mission statements and/or their goals and objectives. Why is this so? And what are the reasons responsible for this?

Evidently, leadership failure, lack of values and commitment, and wrong judgement are some of the reasons ascribed. While I do not contend that these are clearly contributory factors, they are not the only ones. Beyond the obvious reasons already listed, the real reason why organisations fail is largely the result of the inability of managers to divorce their personal vision and goals from those of the organisation. As stated, my views are primarily based on my personal experiences, and so not necessarily applicable to every organisation; however, most organisations are the victims of this inability on the part of their managers.

Even where corporate core values are well defined, there are employees who may not be committed to uphold those values because of their own entrenched motives.

You will agree with me that the formulation and implementation of policies are an essential part of the responsibilities of managers in all organisations. Without managers to enforce them, policies will only be good on paper, as there will be no way of realising the intent through implementation.

However, based on this strategic role, some managers are known to have taken advantage of their privileged position to circumvent official process by subordinating official interest to their personal interest. In other words, they ensure that their personal agendas override the goals and objectives of the organisation.

As a young employee, I had innocently looked forward to my managers and superiors as guiding lights and compasses for organisational direction. I depended upon them, and so I took their views and directives as being the best and most suitable for the organisation, believing their positions were without prejudice and stripped of value judgement. I was wrong.

As I grew in maturity in office administration and imbibed bureaucratic experience, I came to the realisation that not all the views expressed by some of these managers were, for all intents and purposes, in the best interest of the organisation. In fact, some of their judgements were informed and influenced by their personal interests. These were masked in mystery during meetings, where their underhanded motives were indeed wrapped in superior arguments used to influence colleagues who unwittingly failed to discern the subterfuge. Consequently, the personally motivated so-called business decisions were upheld.

In one of the management meetings I attended in a previous place of employment, an important issue came up as to the level of authority that should be given to a particular manager in order to enable him discharge his responsibility outside the head office in Lagos (the capital of Nigeria).

Surprisingly, this decision was guided more by mere petty jealousy than by corporate interest. Because the manager was entitled to certain financial privileges based on the corresponding authority, the merit of the case was downplayed, primarily because he was not trusted or liked by the vocal few. As a result, the meeting reviewed the authority associated with his position as manager, and he was therefore directed to consult with Lagos on issues relating to money before committing the company. Implicitly, the above-referenced manager was now expected to consult with Lagos for all directives and decisions. This meant that the manager would have to travel to Lagos to get a formal approval to dispense any money, the amount notwithstanding. Meanwhile, those behind this decision did not care about the cost implication or the associated risk of having to fly.

In all of this, my own worry was the risk of having to embark on a flight to Lagos anytime there was an issue, incurring logistic challenges and hotel accommodation costs over matters that ordinarily should be within a manager's jurisdiction.

This example illustrates that bureaucratic and political intrigues are endemic to corporation organisations.

Furthermore, these intrigues are recurring devices deployed by some people in the corporate world in order to wield influence and power.

Let's consider another example to illustrate the point even further. A friend of mine once told me of the power play in his organisation. According to him, the deputy managing director had been nursing an ambition to assume the office of the managing director. In order to realise his dream, he used employees loyal to him to set up the incumbent managing director, and, unfortunately, the man fell into the trap set. This eventually led the board to relieve the managing director of his duties, thus paving the way for the deputy to take over responsibilities as the substantive managing director. But, unknown to the board, this decision was the product of the retrogressive plan of the deputy managing director, who had long perfected his plan to take over his boss's position.

In Jeremiah 17:9, God describes man, a product of His creation, as having a deceitful heart and wicked desperation. These words are most instructive, as they warn us to apply all necessary precautionary measures when dealing with our fellow man – and even more so when his heart and deepest desires cannot be known to us.

Even in offices, tea is known to have been used to poison people, leading to redefining the pattern of tea service in the workplace. In one of my former workplaces, tea was served by "office boys" (or girls), as they were called. It was a mobile service, as the boys or girls went from table to table; if employees were not at their desks, the tea was served and covered.

Upon his assumption of duties, a new administrative superintendent stopped the system of serving employees who were not at their desks, highlighting that people were known to have been poisoned through such a method.

This clearly depicts what desperate people in some organisations are capable of doing to eliminate their perceived opponents. As a result, self-service has been introduced in most offices: there is a designated spot where tea, coffee, and other beverages are provided, and employees serve themselves.

Thus, desperation for dominion and unwholesome politicking are part of the reason why some organisations go under, especially after a long period of sustaining such unhealthy practices, all driven by clandestine motives.

Chapter 2

How Personal Vision Overwhelms Corporate Vision

The survival of every organisation or institution, the world over, depends upon a combination of factors, among which are capital, raw materials, manpower, and market. Of these, manpower, or human capital, is arguably the most important. The role of manpower makes it expedient to mention that employees and managers are critical in every segment of the operational chain, and by implication, to the survival of any organisation. No matter how the resources are harnessed, without the human factor encapsulated in the collaboration and cooperation of employees, the vision of the organisation may be scuttled.

Managers in organisations understand this concept, and most of the time, this idea influences their behaviour. Put differently, managers are responsible for policy formulation and implementation, and this entails that they ensure the execution of agreed-upon goals and procedures by their subordinates.

Because of their positions, managers wield considerable influence that permeates all strata of administrative hierarchy in the organisational system. In addition, and also by virtue of their positions, their routine decisions add to the bottom line of any organisation. This means that managers are critical in the value chain throughout the decision-making process.

Based on this insight, some managers are quick to anchor inflated egos fuelled by their perceived importance of their office, which sometimes prompt them to embark on steps that are inimical to company's goals.

As a result, corporate expectations are frustrated, particularly when companies are unable to meet set goals. In this context, the failure could not have been caused by inefficient machinery or inappropriate deployment of resources, including human capital, but only by deliberate human input disproportionate to the overall goal – namely, the aforementioned inappropriate behaviour exhibited by certain managers.

This position is an outcome of the inordinate ambition of some of the personnel occupying strategic positions in the organisation. These are men and women that companies and corporate organisations have entrusted with the responsibility of driving policy formulation and implementation.

Rather than steering this process in a straightforward manner, such individuals introduce extraneous elements, such as office politics and bureaucracy, which further give rise to other unhelpful factors capable of limiting the aspirations of the organisation. This is evident from the behavioural patterns, attitudes, and management styles of those in positions of authority.

When politics, tribalism, ethnicism, and other negative mindsets are introduced into organisations, corporate decisions are hijacked and politicised. In the process, the company, wittingly or unwittingly, becomes vulnerable to undue pressure and influences, thereby commencing a descent into insolvency, and by extension, extinction. When this happens, everybody feels the impact.

For men and women who mean well for a company, once symptoms of politics are observed, it is imperative to speak out and save the careers of all. Once politics in workplaces is not contained, it permeates the entire fabric of the organisation, as it spreading like a deadly virus, with a concomitant effect of polarisation. Depending on the degree of the polarisation, the organisation can be divided into several blocs, or camps, which can create further workplace crises.

Because of their own selfish motives, some managers in organisations opt to create camps. Though these camps are invisible and have no structure, the aim of creating them is to ensure the existence of a crop of dedicated and loyal staff – not necessarily to the company, but to the manager.

The membership of these camps is not documented, nor are formal meetings held, but members who are loyal to a particular "power bloc" know who their cohorts are. This is why elements like promotion, career progression, and even training (whether local or overseas), which ordinarily should be based on organisational needs and predicated on employee merit, is largely determined by the camp to which employees belong.

Chapter 3

Why Oppression Exists in Corporate Organisations

The motives behind the actions of most managers are concealed under blurred circumstances, known only to them, and which they covertly guide. Their identity matrix is not clearly revealed. Sometimes they even appear to have split personalities, making it difficult to situate their character in a definite complex. Implicitly, various elements inform their actions and behaviour. This chapter includes some of these elements but by no means all of them; the list below is not intended to be exhaustive, but it will suffice for the purpose of our discussion.

Religion

Indeed, religion is one of the unseen elements that plays a significant role in the body politic and in corporate organisations.

In Nigeria, decisions are driven and influenced mainly by religious and ethnic considerations. This is deeply rooted among Nigerians, and, unfortunately, this mindset has found its way into the private and public sectors. It now transcends policy decisions and occurs in ordinary day-to-day actions.

Some persons in authority deploy religion as a device to influence or manipulate processes relating to recruitment, promotion, award of contracts, and other organisational policies. Because religion plays a dominant role in matters relating to employment and awarding of contracts, those Nigerians who are desperate to secure favours in these areas from people in authority are prepared to sell their birthright for a bowl of salad. By this I mean that such actions are necessary just for survival purposes. Consequently, some persons are known to have compromised their religious beliefs.

I know of two individuals who had to renounce their faith in exchange for economic opportunity. Both have since reverted to their original religions, having met their objectives. Let's consider these accounts in order to illustrate this point.

The first occurred in Zaria, in 1988, when I was a member of the National Youth Service Corps (NYSC). One Friday, a friend told me that I should accompany him to Jumat service. When I asked if he had converted and was now a Muslim, he told me bluntly that he had indeed converted for fear of joblessness. His motive was to obtain a job by connections with influential Muslims.

Let me provide a bit of background to explain my friend's position. At the time, securing employment was difficult, and this situation was worsened by the Ibrahim Babangida administration's introduction of the Structural Adjustment Programme (SAP) in 1986. The initial effect of the programme was not beneficial to the country, destabilising the economy to the extent that the recruitment capacity of several companies was weakened.

The second instance also involved a person of Christian parentage who had to convert to Islam, in this case, in order to secure accelerated promotion in the armed forces. After retirement, he retraced his steps back to Christianity.

As the preceding examples illustrate, in corporate and other large organisations (such as the government and military), a person's religious leaning is an influential and determining factor in terms of organisational power and decision making. This is particularly evident in Nigeria, a nation with two major competing, or contending, faiths.

Ethnicism

This is another monster that is threatening policies and standards in corporate organisations, including the public sector. In Nigeria, there are more than 250 ethnic groups. However, only three of these groups are sufficient in number to be classified as comprising an ethnic majority: Hausa-Fulani, Yoruba, and Igbo. The others are referred to as minority ethnic groups, based on their small numbers. The three majority ethnic groups thus compete for dominance, both in the public and private sectors.

In most instances, ethnicity is the basis for affinity. Put differently, in all offices, whether public or private, ethnicity is more often than not covertly factored into the decision-making process. During recruiting, the requisite documentation stipulates indicating the applicant's state of origin and local government area. This reveals the ethnic group to which the applicant belongs.

Simply stated, there is a higher level of trust among managers (and recruiters) when dealing with members of their own ethnic group. Along with this comes the justification that "blood is thicker than water", meaning that the bond based on original affiliation is tighter than any other, and increased trust is an extension of that bond.

Some managers invoke and play up this ethnic card in order to perpetuate their hidden agendas. For instance, they will communicate in their native language, rather than in English, as a way of appealing to the sentiments and emotions of surrogates in the same ethnic group as the managers. This tactically confirms that blood is indeed thicker than water, sending signals to these target employees that they need to work together.

Power

In most cases, the lust for power will drive managers to take steps that are inimical to company policy, in an attempt to serve their own individual interests. There is a correlation between authority and power. Persons who occupy positions of authority also have some corresponding level of power and influence in organisations.

In order for some of these managers to remain relevant and hold on to power, they manipulate the system to create an impression of their own indispensability, thereby arrogating gratuitous power for themselves. With this, they transform themselves into epicentres of attraction and relevance.

Employees thus become vulnerable to these managers and their antics, especially those workers who desperately desire to have successful careers in the organisation. Such individuals gravitate to people in authority in order to attract favours that will enable them build their careers, as well as achieve other goals.

Consequently, these employees become willing tools in the hands of self-serving managers. The susceptible among such employees are enlisted and used to perpetuate the hidden agenda of these managers, sometimes with rewards of overseas training and/or promotion or deployment to more juicy positions within the organisation.

Arrogance

Having attained the position of a manager, an individual necessarily becomes part of the organisation's decision-making process. As a result, arrogance often sets in. Arrogant managers exhibit high-handedness and become overbearingly assertive and prideful, particularly towards their subordinates. Furthermore, these managers consider this attitude a strategy for commanding employees' respect – and also courting their friendship – all for the purpose of using these subordinates to serve the managers' own self-serving agendas. And then, if the managers observe that the loyalty of these subordinates has waned or become questionable, they usually dump them in favour of more apt employees.

The reasoning capacity of some of these managers is covered by a false sense of importance which prompts them to perpetually scheme in order to continue to be seen in a positive light by their own superordinates.

Selfishness and Greed

Self-centredness has a firm grip on the psyche of some managers, prompting them to take undue advantage of situations. Their actions are driven by personal desires; that is, within the context of what they will gain for themselves, not necessarily they will achieve for their organisations that they represent.

Owing to self-induced pressures regarding the funding of their own expensive and brazen lifestyles, such managers frequently resort to undermining company policy. For example, a particular manager in a company in Lagos used several false entities (fronts) to submit quotations, disguising them as genuine bidders. Loyal employees then covered the tracks of the fraudulent manager.

Ironically, the fronts submitted several quotations for several companies, all for the same work and with same source of origin. With this, whichever way the pendulum swung, the manager would win the contract through his cronies.

It is this same greed that drives some managers to double-dip in an organisation. For example, by virtue of their positions, managers are entitled to status cars, which they are officially required to use for company assignments. Rather than subordinate themselves to this regulation, they elect to draw from pool cars for official assignments.

Implicitly, jobs suffer, as subordinates from the same department as the manager are not able to deploy official cars from the pool for official duties, resulting in the failure to meet deadlines. Ironically, in the midst of all this, the manager, who is the head of the department, uses for personal matters the same car meant for the department's official use, leaving the subordinates who are not bold enough to question this act to suffer. Not to mention that the productivity of the department and organisation will suffer as well.

This action, no doubt, is a clear violation of company policy, which requires managers to use their status cars for official duties. This they are expected to do until the end of four years' time, when the car reverts to them through a process of repurchase at zero book value.

The underpinning motive behind these managers' actions is aimed at ensuring that the cars in question remain new and in very good condition for the time when the managers will take full ownership of the vehicles.

Ambition

Some managers have immoderate ambition driven by their desire to rise astronomically to the top; some even set their sights on becoming the managing director, or holding another top position, and then fixate on attaining that goal. With this in mind, they gradually work their way to the top through evil plots. Often, such individuals plant moles from among members of their cabal in the system in order to sabotage and plot the downfall of their superiors, thereby creating openings that then enable their elevation to the desired position. This is why it is absolutely necessary to always watch your back in an organisation; some ambitious elements may be scheming to frustrate your efforts for their own selfish purposes.

Fear of the Unknown

The majority of those who amass wealth through dubious methods will tell you that their actions are informed by the need to secure their future, mainly because of fear of the unknown. For instance, they have to contend with job insecurity, socio-economic woes, an unreliable pension scheme, etc.

Therefore, to secure their future, they use their loyalists in the system in order to plot ways of maximising every instance that will translate into their own positive opportunities and/or increased status in the organisation.

Money

Money is key in our quest for comfort. This is the reason why it is pursued all over the world by men and women who desire comfort. The quest for currency brings out ingenuity in man. In some organisations, besides the remuneration and other entitlements, some managers make sure they generate opportunities within the system that will translate to money. Their desire for money is insatiable, and since they do not know where to draw the line, they compromise their office and outwit corporate rules.

Beyond the silky-smooth suits and dresses which make some managers conjure a pure and respectable image, the hearts and minds are filled with unhealthy thoughts. Thoughts that are directed towards taking advantage of colleagues, subordinates, and the system – all for the managers' own selfish ends. Because of their desire to rise, become powerful, and earn ever more money, they use their positions to frustrate the careers of those subordinates who refuse to cooperate and join their unholy network.

These are some of the factors that have singly or collectively driven some managers in various organisations to embark on hidden agendas. As such, these factors shape decision making. Specifically, during meetings where decisions are made on some specific issues, these managers' attitudes and behavioural patterns, as well as the nature of their contributions, are shaped by these factors.

Companies or corporate organisations with solid potential, and those that have shown enviable promise for growth, are known to have collapsed, receded into deficit, insolvency, or stunted growth, or barely survived. These are some of the consequences of the actions of a few men and women who have chosen to chart a course of action in line with their personal ambition, at the expense of the progress of the company.

It does not matter to these employees occupying prominent positions and consequently saddled with important responsibilities – namely, managers – whether their actions are at variance with the policy of their organisations or not. They are not bothered by the consequences. Instead of engaging in deep strategic thinking that could boost company objectives, their primary preoccupation is to bring their hidden agendas to bear, thus achieving their inordinate desire for power, money, and all that accompanies having them. Once they have accomplished this, they realise that their objectives have indeed been achieved, and so they feel fulfilled, prompting them to exhibit signs of ecstasy.

All over the world, corporate organisations groan under the suffocating influence of managers who are supposed to provide leadership, but, instead, only serve their own ends. They abound in every organisation, asserting their influence to achieve their aims. Deep down they are not concerned about the damaging effects to the psyches of their staff, nor are they bothered by the impact on the organisation.

A particular manager in one of the organisations where I worked was always reluctant to take his annual vacation. Even when he was compelled to proceed, he made sure that the delegation of authority (DOA) he assigned to his next in command was exclusive of some specific responsibility. He then gave counter-directives to those of the DOAs holder during his absence. The reason for this behaviour was to ensure the manager's uninterrupted relevance in the system. It was a strategy for sustaining his contacts for delivery of his self-serving planned motives.

To close this chapter, let us just say that such managers have no conscience and are detrimental to every organisation, and yet they abound worldwide.

Chapter 4

Tactics Deployed to Execute Selfish Ambition

Rewards, Threats, and Blackmail

In their quest to achieve their objectives, managers deploy rewards or threats, depending on which seems more potent and most effective in compelling employee loyalty, given the specific circumstances.

Employees with immoderate ambition are willing tools for manipulation. These are the employees whom such managers carefully identify and then lure through reward and/or threat, as described above.

The managers begin their plans in the departments or divisions which comprise their primary sphere of influence. The nucleus of employees used by these managers is drawn from their departments or division.

In the departments under their jurisdiction, the extent to which staff can rise in their own career pinnacle is dependent upon the managers' whims and caprices. During performance evaluation and appraisal exercises, these managers determine the scores and the promotions merited, along with the training required, whether local or foreign.

Employees who have demonstrated unflinching support and loyalty are identified and admitted into an "inner circle" which serves as a camp for the propagation of the managers' crude desires. For you to grow in career, you must belong to a camp. Those who opt to maintain a neutral or non-aligned position, based on principle, have their careers sacrificed on the altar of integrity.

With a clear understanding of the foregoing, members of these camps are commissioned to execute some of the unholy agendas at their workplaces. They are used as moles, and part of the mission is to track the activities of staff considered to be obstacles in the way of these managers. Unbeknown to the innocent and unsuspecting employees, they are put under surveillance by sycophants.

Tactics employed in monitoring the perceived enemy employees include snooping into the official or private affairs of staff they consider inimical to their managers' aspirations. The managers, through the moles they have planted in other departments, monitor development in these departments, including these activities of fellow managers. Thus, unbeknown to these other managers, their activities are monitored by their colleagues.

Blackmail is a formidable tool, and scheming managers use it in the pursuit of their illicit intentions. Blackmail will ensure that the schemers get the cooperation of their fellow managers (i.e. the ones spied upon), particularly those identified as threats or potential threats to the self-serving managers' ambitions in the organisation.

These self-serving, scheming managers also keep close tabs on their fellow managers in order to discover possible violations of company rules. This creates yet another opportunity for blackmail, whether it forces their colleagues into submission, cooperation, or collaboration. The mole employee loyal to these dubious managers continually provide them with feedback, and the evil managers in turn process the outcomes to use for further exploitation.

No matter the organisation, watch your back at all times, and be especially careful to discern and guard against the moles in your midst.

Chapter 5

Impact on Career Growth

The professional destiny of most employees is conditioned by the preferences of their bosses, particularly in a system where the management relies on the opinion of those bosses to determine their career growth. Promotions in most organisations are based on the annual appraisal system.

This is where goals are set for the employees, within the scope of their schedule of duties, and their individual performance is then examined against the backdrop of corporate objectives. The goals have delivery time frames against which assessments are made as to whether said goals have been met or exceeded.

In the course of this evaluation, performance is rated, and this further determines which employees qualify for promotions and bonuses. Skill gaps are identified and determined in the course of the evaluation as well, with a view to making recommendations as to specific relevant training required to address the shortfall.

On paper, the system appears to be good, but in reality, it is a mechanism for victimisation. Indeed, it is a trap used by some managers to victimise their subordinates considered disloyal or not in their "good books". Some managers remind their subordinates of pending appraisals as a strategy to secure their loyalty. The careers of some employees have been cut short by commission, omission, or elimination.

Put differently, some managers use the appraisal system to the detriment of their subordinates. Employees who are not in the good books of their managers pay dearly in terms of their careers, as their bosses ensure that they receive low marks on their assessments so that their performance ratings do not earn them promotions or bonuses. And then, based on the low rating, which implies the employees require further training to boost their skills, the managers ensure that these subordinates are listed for local training. (Such managers frustrate every justification for foreign training.)

Through this appraisal process, careers are frustrated, as victims begin to experience career stagnation. That is why some employees remain on one group level for ten to fifteen years, or more, without promotion.

Chapter 6

Impact on Contract Decisions

In all organisations, there are procedures for the award of contracts. These procedures are designed to promote best practices, where only qualified contractors with the required competence are pre-qualified and subsequently awarded contracts after due fulfilment of the requirements. Emphasis is also placed on transparency, fairness, and accountability in the process.

The foregoing is mainly to ensure that the process is not compromised or manipulated in favour of particular contractors. It is also to guide against insider abuse, where those privy to the rules communicate such information to their favoured contractors or clients, thereby giving them undue advantage. In addition, it is also to prevent managers from taking advantage of the system by awarding contracts to themselves through cronies or relatives.

The procedures for awarding contracts comprise the ideal situation. In practical terms, however, some of these rules are deliberately breached by some managers with nefarious motives. Contracts worth millions or even billions of naira or dollars are deliberately influenced in favour of their friends or companies where they have vested interests. For these managers, company policy – not to mention personal and professional ethics – mean nothing. The policy itself is nothing more than a piece of paper which can covertly be violated.

In one of these companies, there was a particular general manager who used his firms to bid for jobs in the company where he was supposed to superintend, using cronies as fronts. He used the loyal staff in his department to facilitate the exercise, and as the boss in the department, nobody could put him under any check system.

As a result, firms belonging to the general manager came to the top of the list during the technical and commercial stages of the bid. With the aid of his insider knowledge, the bids were better packaged, containing all the required details and information, and thereby putting his companies ahead of others. In some cases, the focal persons in the department were sent to lobby members of the tender's board to ensure their bids would be successful.

However, some bids would go to the minor tender's board because of their financial size. (This process is more vulnerable to abuse because there are fewer checks in the system.) Corrupt managers would often take advantage of the process, submitting more than one quotation. In fact, the same person might submit five quotations, with each one packaged as coming from a different source.

The foregoing is not the rule but the exception, as several bids also pass through the bidding process without being compromised, to the extent that their companies have no insider interest. In other words, where no vested interest in any of the competitive bids exists, judgements are not manipulated, and the most qualified bidder receives the job.

When procedures and processes are breached, the major consequences are that integrity and transparency are compromised, and best practices are undermined, resulting in poor-quality work, fake materials, inferior goods, and inefficient delivery of services.

The company eventually suffers from this unhealthy process, including frequent breakdown of machinery, other goods, and services, with severe financial implications on the company's balance sheet, brand management, and reputation.

Chapter 7

Impact on Organisational Growth

The growth of any organisation is contingent upon the quality of decisions taken by its management. In most cases, companies whose decisions are driven by the prejudices of employees (usually managers) face challenges capable of overwhelming the organisation. Companies known to have demonstrated potential for growth nosedive under the weight of such unhealthy practices.

One company started on a strong note at its inception. The operational philosophy was excellent. The management style was encouraging and reassuring. The recruitment process was fantastic, as it focused on qualifying capable personnel with technical know-how. It was at this point that some of us were recruited into the organisation, with a high sense of career esteem and aspirations.

However, as time went on, mediocrity and other unhealthy extraneous forces took over. Policies that were ordinarily designed to guide the processes and operations of the company began to give way to a value system characterised by preconceived notions, prejudices, predispositions, selfishness, and corruption. Procedures were circumvented, and because the chief executive officer failed to lead by example, everybody suffered, including the company.

For instance, a time came when the CEO lost sight of his core responsibilities, concentrating instead on matters that were not of critical importance to the future of the organisation. In the name of marketing, he would globetrot, gallivant, and deploy company resources in erroneous use, sometimes through questionable processes. As a result, other members of executive management, seeing what was happening but lacking the moral courage to confront the CEO, began to help themselves through unhealthy processing aimed at enriching their own personal fortunes.

This development subsequently permeated the system to the extent that even those at the lower rungs of management strata, as well as other senior and junior staff, took advantage of the corrupt system and indulged in unhealthy practices that were antithetical to the good of the organisation. Soon, initial hope of a prosperous company with a bright future and career growth gave way to despair and frustration, as things began to fall apart.

Cost to the Organisation

Like every other organisation, the cost was enormous. Productivity declined, and employee morale dwindled, resulting in a high labour turnover and a loss of skilled employees. Eventually, a negative public perception of the company emerged.

Shareholders had their shares wiped out or eroded. Management and staff fell from their high horses, losing their positions, career opportunities, and aspirations.

Contractors were not spared either, as some were unable to obtain payment for work executed.

This example illustrates why it is fundamentally important to pool the energies of all employees who desire to make their companies survive so that they can achieve their career dreams.

Chapter 8

Overcoming Career Oppression

When you remain focused in regard to anything you set out to accomplish, whether professional or private, you can easily manage distractions.

Know Your Onions

Most people join an organisation as experienced hires, based on a particular skill, while others join as graduate trainees or from the bottom of the organisational ladder. In whatever capacity you operate, ensure you discharge your responsibility with utmost competence by focusing on your job. This will make it difficult for your manager or boss to plot your downfall.

Once you demonstrate capacity beyond doubt, showing that indeed you are on top of your responsibilities, it becomes difficult to frustrate you, and even if your rivals do manage to get to you, it will only be for a short duration, as your competence will act as a buffer and defence mechanism against underhanded motives.

There was a particular manager who tried to enlist an employee into his camp in order to get feedback on the goings-on in the department to which this employee belonged. The employee quietly declined by consistently refusing to pass on any information concerning his department to the scheming manager.

As a result, the underhanded manager opposed the employee's promotion during deliberations at the management committee level. However, the majority of committee members supported the employee's elevation on grounds of competence, which they said had been observed over time and across the board. Consequently, the manager was constrained from carrying out his vindictive action against the employee.

This example illustrates why it is important to ensure you are not found wanting in terms of fulfilling your job responsibilities, as your enemies can use that to plot your downfall in the workplace.

Abide by and Operate within Company Rules

In every organisation, there are rules and regulations that guide the operations and business of the company. Processes and procedures of the company, as well as general conduct of employees, are regulated with appropriate limits clearly defined by these policies.

These policies vary from company to company, but the common ones which are critical to any management are those relating to health, safety, and environment (HSE); business ethics; conflicts of interest; and criminal acts. These policies, which state broad terms and scope of compliance, also make provisions for violations and/or breaches, including the corresponding penalties for such actions.

It is therefore advised for employees, particularly those who do not want to be caught in the political intrigue of the company, to study these policies upon assumption of duty and thereafter ensure strict compliance. Once you maintain adherence, it becomes difficult for your detractors in the system to set you up or apply the policies against you to establish any sort of guilt.

For you to experience a crisis-free career, you must make observance of these policies an article of faith. You must resist any temptation that may make you breach these policies in breach. This is important because once you have demonstrated leadership qualities, intelligence, and capabilities that are superior to those of your boss (i.e. direct manager/supervisor) or other persons in leadership positions, you will also have unwittingly made yourself a candidate for envy, and as such, you may be marked for destruction by those in position of authority and/or their minions.

Update Your Knowledge and Skills to Make Yourself Indispensable

One good way to insulate yourself from the political intrigues of any office environment, and simultaneously protect your job, is to demonstrate competence to a level of indispensability (or as close to that as possible). You can attain this level by acquiring knowledge and skills that will put you ahead of your colleagues or peers.

This can be done by privately enrolling in courses or training relevant to your field of work. In addition, you can also extensively use the Internet to access information that can help you develop your knowledge and skills. The Internet has made this process much easier, as a gamut of information is now at your fingertips. Indeed, there is no information that cannot be found on the Internet. People with little education have increased their knowledge through the use and proper application of the Internet. Today, in terms of intelligence, capability, spoken and written expression, and other comparable measurements of competency, they are practically indistinguishable from holders of doctoral degrees.

Thus, you must not be discouraged by the cost or effort necessary to acquire additional knowledge and skills. By sacrificing your time, finances, and other resources, you are investing positively in your future. Your future is in your hands, and the shape and outcome of it depends upon how much commitment you have made to keep it in line with your desires and aspirations.

Plus, such investment will help you demonstrate capacity beyond doubt. And when you are seen in your organisation to have demonstrated capacity beyond doubt, even a boss who has pencilled you down will be constrained to decide against you, as he or she will wish to avoid the labelling of oppressive manager, by both colleagues and superordinates.

If you are truly capable beyond doubt – and, better yet, indispensable – not even a network of conspiracies, sabotage, and betrayal by your detractors in an organisation can scale through without detection as targeted oppression. Implicitly, by means of your exceptional competence, you will automatically neutralise such schemes, rendering virtually ineffectual the trappings and evil plans against you.

One employee was consistently marked down by his boss as a ploy to deprive him of promotion, and for about ten years the employee was never promoted. Nevertheless, he remained unruffled, never letting frustration get the better of him, even when his juniors were elevated above him and became his superiors.

On one particular day, each employee's case was presented to management for final consideration at the end of the annual appraisal exercise. This same employee was marked down by his boss, as usual. But his decision was overruled by other members of the management team, with each attesting to the employee's competence as consistently demonstrated, even beyond the departmental level. On the strength of this, he was promoted – against the wishes of his manager, of course.

This example clearly demonstrates that you can be what you want to be, and with just a little push, you will attain your desired outcomes.

Maintain a Position of Nonalignment

Upon assumption of duty in any organisation, do not make friends hastily. It is essential to create what we can call an "observation period", during which time you observe the organisation, the people, the policies, the style of implementation, the office culture, and, if possible, the attitudes and thought processes of the people.

There is a saying in my native language that when a bird gets to a new place, it stands on one leg until it is familiar with the environment; only then does it stand on both legs. This perfectly illustrates the principle of using the observation period. The observation period is important because both your career and peace of mind in the workplace depend on it.

Even when employees come around and make overtures of friendship, endeavour to keep them at arm's length so that you can properly observe them, particularly in regard to their intentions. Some of them are moles spying for dubious managers. Their aim is to win you over, get you into their camp, and force you to do their bidding, all of which is obviously antithetical and inimical to company policy, ethics, and well-being.

Give attention to your job, and pool your energy and resources towards ensuring that your career will flourish. The key to having a successful career is the proof of competence that will shield you from the web of sycophancy in which people of average intelligence, competence, and ability congregate in order to survive.

Just a few more thoughts on sycophants. Sycophants are usually people of average intelligence who lack confidence and delivery capacity. In any system, they continually look for means of covering up their deficiencies, thereby becoming vulnerable to manipulation by those in authority. In corporate organisations, sycophants are negative and destructive elements deployed by dubious managers for their own selfish purposes.

Build Relationships Only with Trustworthy People

Relationship building is important in any organisation, and key to the spirit of teamwork, as it opens people to new ideas and knowledge. One simple way of building relationships is through information sharing, which can be accomplished through interaction and bridge-building among colleagues.

While this is important, remember the caveats throughout this book! Interact and build bridges with only those who are not entangled in internal politics. You must avoid those who backstab, destroy, condemn, gossip, and even flatter people in organisations. These are the sycophants of the organisation. To repeat and re-emphasise, you must avoid such people. They are dangerous and pose a serious threat to your career. Their motives are wrapped in secrecy, and you must remain vigilant in order to avoid their traps.

If you seek to network, make friends, build bridges, and interact – which, admittedly, is important for teamwork – do so with people of impeccable character, people with a high sense of integrity, people who have the fear of God in them.

An easy-going young man in one organisations fell victim to the vices of these sycophants and ended up ruining his career. It all started when, upon the assumption of his duties, he tried to make friends with the people who came his way. In the process, political enemies within the system captured him, enlisting him into the camp of a particular manager outside his department.

This development did not go down well with his own manager, who felt his loyalty was in doubt because he was now seen as a mole potentially relating information to his new friend (the dubious manager of the other department). As a result, his own manager contacted the human resources manager, saying that he should be transferred to another department. The reason the manager gave was that the employee could not be trusted with classified documents and information.

A few months later, after he'd been transferred to another department, the employee received a letter from

HR declaring him redundant; subsequently, he lost his job. This would have been avoided if he had taken the time to study the people and environment (observation period) before building bridges with people he knew little or nothing about.

Once again, making friends in the workplace is good, but you must always look carefully before leaping. In most organisations, there are people who backstab to get favours. You must avoid these elements at all costs. Get to know who is who and what is what before you become allied with the wrong people and find yourself an unwitting victim of dubious managers and their schemes and sycophant agents.

Avoid Cutting Corners

You must avoid the easy but unprofessional, unethical, and anomalous ways of getting things done. A lot of people have the erroneous belief that by cutting corners in an organisation, they will be seen as smart guys, especially if service delivery through such methods could result in a shorter time frame.

Always abide by the rules, regulations, and policies of your organisation in the course of discharging your responsibilities. Let no man put you under pressure to circumvent the officially approved process of carrying out your duties. If you breach procedures, and the outcome fails to meet the expectations of those you are trying to impress or who have deceived you into executing said breach, you will be held accountable and face the consequences alone.

Some people even cut corners through falsification. This is a criminal offence, and the penalty in any organisation is dismissal with ignominy. Criminal charges from law enforcement may ensue as well.

Consider a young man with a promising career who worked in one of the hospitals owned by the state petroleum company. He was in the dispensing unit where drugs were issued to patients. On account of frequent out-of-stock notices to patients, the unit came under investigation. It turned out that the employee in question had been diverting the pharmaceuticals under his watch in the dispensing unit. This was all for his own personal commercial motives, of course, and he was consequently dismissed from service.

Twenty years after this incident, this man still lives in a rented apartment, soliciting for support from friends. Whereas those with whom he started work are now landlords. This example begs the question, why take shortcuts if you will end up being the loser? The money he received from selling the drugs he stole did not compare to the ongoing financial setback he had to sustain because of losing his job and ruining his professional reputation.

Focus on and Trust in God

Dependence on God in all your endeavours means total surrender and complete submission to His will. Because He is the omniscient, omnipotent, and omnipresent God, He is aware of our limitations, abilities, circumstances, experiences, and challenges. Therefore, in order to survive in any environment in which you find yourself, you must go to Him for solutions, protection, and wisdom, through prayers and supplication.

Relying on, leaning on, and depending upon dubious managers for protection in an organisation is recipe for failure. Keeping company with those managers will only give you temporary relief and a false sense of protection and hope, to the extent they are able to use their positions to influence promotions and attract other benefits to you, including overseas training. These managers are really Greeks bearing gifts, so to speak, and you should beware. Such gifts are designed to sustain your allegiance to them and manipulate you into executing their unholy deeds. The day you do things considered inimical to their wishes, they will extract a pound of your flesh and abandon you in the middle of nowhere. Most certainly, it will be the beginning of your step onto the precipice of frustration in such an organisation.

God has warned that we should avoid the company of such persons. As Proverbs 13:20 says, "He that walked with wise men shall be wise: but a companion of fools shall be destroyed."

What we see in society today is a reversal of God's directive. Relationships are built based on economic survival. We are unable to stand up to our superordinates and bosses and tell them the truth, for fear of victimisation and job loss.

So, in an attempt to survive, we compromise by collaborating with our bosses to perpetuate evil in corporate organisations. It does not matter to us whether our actions are in line with biblical principles or not. What matters is whether our decisions advance our careers. Embarking on such a path leads to ruin, so avoid it at all costs.

Safeguard Your Reputation by Maintaining Discipline and Dignity

Part of the power play in the corporate world is the strategy of weakening the reputations of perceived enemies and bringing them to ridicule. Dubious individuals know that once you lose the respect of your colleagues, you become vulnerable, and people will believe any charges made against you. It is therefore imperative that you safeguard your reputation by maintaining your dignity and displaying a high level of discipline within the system, as this is the best way to avoid the traps they set.

The most common landmines underhanded managers deploy to bring down their perceived enemies in the system include contract manipulation (and inflating various other costs and expenses) and sexual harassment, both of which we will discuss below.

Many great men in various organisations have fallen victim to contract manipulation, not because they were not intelligent or smart, but because they were not disciplined enough. Of particular in interest is the managing director of one organisation. Upon his assumption of duties, he wanted to enthrone a system that would encourage excellence and eliminate mediocrity and indolence.

Unfortunately, people generally are not amenable to change. Those who profit from the abnormal system want to ensure the status quo which enables them to perpetuate their evil plans. Such was the case in this organisation.

As a result, the managing director was set up by means of an inflated contract which he knew nothing about. Thinking the deal in question were in the best interest of the company, the new managing director signed the contract. The cabal in the system then went around and petitioned the head office. Even the investigation panel set up to look into the situation was mostly comprised of members of the cabal, resulting in the sacking of the managing director.

Therefore, guarding against manipulation is imperative. If you are disciplined, you will already have won half the battle.

Next, let's consider sexual harassment. Another pathetic story will provide our illustrative example. A manager had to resign his job prematurely in order to take up a new job in the organisation in question. His new position was head of the human resources department. Given his wealth of experience, he observed that there were a lot of gaps in the system that would have to be closed up as part of a strategy to strengthen and reposition the company.

He confidentially told a few employees about his plans to overhaul the HR policies. Unbeknown to him, some of the employees he confided in gave feedback to the cabal in the system. These individuals already felt threatened that they would lose the hold they had on HR, through which they influenced recruitment.

To sabotage the new HR head, they set him up, using a beautiful young married lady in the same department. Unfortunately, because of his lack of self-discipline, he fell prey to the antics of the young lady, who pretended to be in love with him. When he attempted to reciprocate the advances of the young lady, the new HR head was quickly reported to executive management, with allegations of sexual harassment.

The committee set up to investigate the matter noted with disappointment the conduct of the new HR head. For such allegations to have been made, there had to have been elements of truth to them, and given his high position as head of HR, his conduct was supposed to serve as an exemplar of moral standards. Thus, he was relieved of his duties.

This example shows that lack of self-discipline inevitably has negative repercussions that result in unavoidable devastating effects on careers.

Dress Modestly

One way to exhibit discipline and dignity is to dress modestly. What you wear no doubt speaks volume about your personality. People who dress neatly in public are generally considered to be neat people, even at home; hence it is important to maintain a demeanour of neatness. Those who overdress wittingly or unwittingly attract undue attention to themselves, and this in turn may earn the wrath of a direct manager who is not a good dresser. It is best to dress modestly, particularly if you have a manager who does not appreciate a good sense of fashion.

A friend of mine who was fond of dressing splendidly soon became a source of envy among some of his colleagues. Based on this, they went as far as insinuating that he was devoting too much of his time to fashion, at the expense of his work. Even though they were unable to prove how that had affected his productivity, his boss maliciously used this to contain his career. My friend eventually resigned from the organisation out of frustration.

In a corporate setting, those with poor dress habits will be the first to criticise you, attributing your dress style to laziness, nonchalance, and lack of commitment to the job – an insinuation induced by envy, simply because you outshine them.

Do Not Publicise Your Extracurricular Activities or Achievements

Another way to exhibit discipline and dignity is to avoid boasting about extracurricular work activities. In some parts of the world, it is normal for people to have more than one paying job. In Nigeria, for example, people who take up paid employment in either the public or private sector generally do not engage in other jobs, not because they are not interested, but because are constrained by time. However, there are those who brave the odds to take up part-time jobs or to apply their skills for the purpose of generating additional income to augment their earnings. Such people usually exhibit a disposition of financial freedom and contentment, as they are able to meet their financial needs, pursue their dreams, and, most of the time, execute their projects.

Never allow your colleagues or bosses to know that you engage in such extracurricular activities, as this could be used against you by your detractors in the system – once again out of envy. Some malicious colleagues or bosses may want to pull you down through a campaign of calumny, alleging that you have used company resources for personal gain or that your productivity has been negatively affected by your extracurricular activities. They may even imply that your secondary source of legitimate work is some sort of unseemly private engagement.

Such circumstances led a friend of mine to lose his lucrative job in the oil sector. He took up writing as an avocation, and he authored several books, some of which became best sellers. This provoked envy. When his company embarked upon a restructuring programme, he became a victim, losing his job in the exercise. His boss and some other key employees in the organisation never liked the media attention and fame he enjoyed in the public space on account of his literary works.

Therefore, discipline, dignity, and discretion are the best practices to follow in every organisation.

Conclusion

Most people dream of having a career in the corporate world because of the promises it holds in terms of opportunities. However, upon employment, the bliss of this long-held dream soon fades as the emerging realities run contrary to expectations. For young employees, early detection of the symptoms of corporate politics is remote, as they are overwhelmed by their new status as staff of a large organisation. Put differently, the euphoria of the dream is real, but the actual environment is bogus.

As time goes by, the stark realities come more clearly into focus. Even the most innocent young employees eventually discover the truth about the sinister and dishonest people with whom they must work, including their evil minds and malicious strategies. As reality sets in that this is the environment in which they are expected to work in order to achieve their career goals, they inevitably realise that their dreams of career fulfilment are nothing more than a delusion.

Those determined to survive the politics in any organisation will quickly adjust to their surroundings. Furthermore, they identify with the political bloc they consider appropriate to give them the protection necessary for them to attain their goals. Others strictly adhere to their integrity and moral standards, never playing the political game. The choice is strictly individual. As we have seen throughout this book, there is always the option to remain neutral and concentrate on professional responsibility, letting indispensable competence and impeccable character speak for themselves. This option seems the best one, as it usually wins the day in the end, with individual preserving his or her reputation, integrity, and self-respect.

Let us look at one final example. A fellow in one organisation opted to align with his boss's camp, but when the boss ran into trouble in that same organisation, the management board not only relieved the boss of his job, they also sacked all those considered to be his ardent loyalists, including this fellow. It was indeed an eye-opener for a lot of others in the organisation at that time, as it highlighted the risk of wading into the murky waters of corporate politics.

Perhaps the reason why some people lavishly celebrate retirement is the relief of not experiencing a major hitch during a thirty-odd-year career of unbroken and meritorious service. Not everybody is lucky enough to experience a smooth ride in their career journeys. Some careers are cut short prematurely, either by means of arranged indictment of a criminal offence or because of death. Not everybody comes out alive after a stint in an organisation. Some lucky ones even end up in hospital, diagnosed with various types of diseases.

Therefore, do not be carried away by the stunning appearance of people in the workplace. Most times, these good looks can be deceitful, as those you see, no matter how close they are to you, may be satanic agents in human clothing. If you think that nothing can be harmful when you put all your trust in a man in a corporate organisation, think again.

You must learn to put your trust in God, who already knows your end from the beginning, with a clear insight as to what you will become even while in your mother's womb. He promised to supply all your needs, and His grace is sufficient for you; hence you should not trouble yourself over anything.